5/11

Ripley's Believe It or Not!

Developed and produced by Ripley Publishing Ltd

This edition published and distributed by:
Mason Crest Publishers Inc.
370 Reed Road, Broomall, Pennsylvania 19008
(866) MCP-BOOK (toll free)
www.masoncrest.com

Ripley's Believe it or Not!
Curious Creations
ISBN 978-1-4222-2017-7 (hardcover)
ISBN 978-1-4222-2051-1 (paperback)
Library of Congress Cataloging-in-Publication data is available

Ripley's Believe it or Not!—Complete 16 Title Series
ISBN 978-1-4222-2014-6

1st printing
10 9 8 7 6 5 4 3 2 1

Library of Congress Cataloging-in-Publication Data is available.
Printed in USA

PUBLISHER'S NOTE
While every effort has been made to verify the accuracy of the entries in this book, the Publisher's cannot be held responsible for any errors contained in the work. They would be glad to receive any information from readers.

WARNING
Some of the stunts and activities in this book are undertaken by experts and should not be attempted by anyone without adequate training and supervision.

Ripley's Believe It or Not!

The Remarkable... Revealed

CURIOUS CREATIONS

Mason Crest Publishers

CURIOUS CREATIONS

Amazing art. Prepare to be stunned by unbelievable sculptures and art from all over the world. Discover the plastic wrap figures that mysteriously appear on the streets of Washington, D.C, the dotty artwork that makes people see spots before their eyes in Sydney, Australia, and the bike that looks like a burger in Hyderabad, India.

Heather Jansch of Devon, England, makes incredible driftwood sculptures of horses...

DRIFTWOOD HORSES

Heather Jansch of Devon, England, makes incredible sculptures of horses... from old pieces of wood that are washed up on beaches.

She had the idea for creating driftwood artworks when her son, looking for wood for a fire, chopped a piece of ivy that had grown around a fencing stake. He left behind a section that she thought would make a good horse's torso for the copper wire sculpture on which she was working. She makes both small and life-size equine sculptures. Her larger sculptures have a steel frame, which is coated with

Each of Heather's sculptures can be months in the making. Sometimes they are left incomplete while Heather searches for the right pieces of wood to complete the jigsaw.

fiberglass to roughen it up and stop the wood from slipping, as it would do on bare metal. When Heather is happy with the position of the pieces of driftwood, they are tied with wire and then screwed together to hold them in place. The animals' hooves are made from old copper immersion heater tanks. As she usually places her finished works in natural, outdoor environments, such as fields, they must be self-supporting and sturdy enough to cope with high winds without falling over. And for exhibitions, they need to be able to withstand being lifted by crane. Heather's biggest problem is a lack of driftwood. Her full-size sculptures require a number of pieces from which she selects the best. She often has to travel miles to find suitable specimens.

Heather finds the driftwood for her sculptures on beaches after high tides and storms.

GHOST SHIP

When a 29-ft (8.8-m) yacht sailed from Fair Isle, Shetland, to Newcastle upon Tyne, England, in July 2005 (a journey of 330 mi/ 530 km), there was something missing— a crew. For this was the Ghost Ship, the brainchild of Boston, Massachusetts, artist Chris Burden, who wanted to create a crewless, self-navigating yacht. Built in Southampton, England, the boat was controlled via onboard computers but, just in case it ran into trouble, it was shadowed by an accompanying support vessel throughout the five-day voyage.

CHOCOLATE BUST

New York artist Janine Antoni made a series of self-portrait busts in soap and chocolate. For her chocolate creations, she chisels cubes of chocolate with her teeth. Antoni once used the brainwave signals recorded while she dreamed at night as a pattern for weaving a blanket the following morning. And for a 1992 exhibition she washed her long hair and then mopped the floor of an art gallery in London, England, with it!

MIGHTY MURAL

Since the 1970s, thousands of artists have contributed to a huge mural on the banks of a river at Pueblo, Colorado. The mural, which officially measures 2 mi (3.2 km) long and 58 ft (18 m) high, contains portraits of the likes of Elvis Presley, Andy Warhol, and Bob Marley, and contributors are invited to add to it each year.

EMPTY FEELING

British artist David Hensel was surprised when his sculpture was rejected by a leading art show—and even more so when its empty base was accepted and displayed on its own! The judges at the Royal Academy's Summer Exhibition thought the statue—a laughing head—and base were separate works. And they much preferred the base, complete with its piece of wood sticking up that was meant to keep the head in place.

△ PAVEMENT PICASSO

British artist Julian Beever creates incredible 3-D chalk drawings on flat city sidewalks. Known as the "Pavement Picasso," he has chalked pictures in America, Europe, and Australia, including a swimming pool so lifelike that shoppers swerved to avoid it and Coca-Cola bottles that appear to spring out of the ground. In a street in London, England, in 2006, the artist starred in his own work by posing against a wall (perched on a ledge he had drawn), while waiting to be rescued from a burning building by Batman and Robin!

PAPER SHIP

Jared Shipman of Roseville, California, built a 320,000-piece model, 9 ft (2.7-m) long, of the USS *Nimitz,* out of paper.

FAKE COLLECTION

Christophe Petyt of Paris, France, founded L'Art du Faux, a collection of more than 3,500 fake masterpieces. He has 82 artists working for him re-creating old masters. Visitors to Petyt's exhibitions have included Arnold Schwarzenegger, Frank Sinatra, and La Toya Jackson.

AMPHIBIOUS TRAILER

From 1989, Rick Dobbertin of Syracuse, New York, spent 4½ years (14,000 man-hours) turning an old milk trailer into a 32-ft (10-m) long stainless steel amphibious craft in which he hoped to circumnavigate the Earth over land and sea. He didn't quite achieve his objective, but he did manage to travel more than 33,000 mi (53,100 km) on land and a further 3,000 mi (4,828 km) on the ocean, tackling seas that swelled up to 18 ft (5.5 m) in the process.

SHARK WATCH

The Pentagon is hoping to use remote-controlled sharks as possible spies. U.S. engineers have created a neural implant—a series of electrodes embedded into the brain—that is designed to enable the signals of a shark's brain to be manipulated remotely. They plan to test the device on blue sharks off the coast of Florida.

BLIND DEVOTION

For more than 30 years, John Cook has created masterpieces in wood. But the Tennessee man never gets to see the finished product—because he is blind. Although he lost his sight to glaucoma as a child, Cook uses a measuring stick and gage blocks with brail markings to produce beautifully intricate furniture. Each cut he makes is steady, deliberate, and perfect. "My hands are my eyes," he explains.

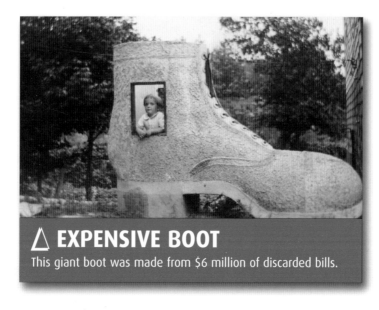

⚠ EXPENSIVE BOOT

This giant boot was made from $6 million of discarded bills.

WOODEN 'GATOR

In 2005, Michael Smith of Baton Rouge, Louisiana, made a solid toothpick alligator from about three million toothpicks! He has also made a wearable hat, a saxophone, a fully functional briefcase, and delicate butterflies—all from common toothpicks.

TALL TOPIARY

In 1983, Moirangthem Okendra Kumbi began turning a Duranta hedge plant into a giant topiary. The plant, which he calls "Sweetheart," now stands a huge 61 ft (19 m) tall in Manipur, India. He spends five hours a day clipping, feeding, and watering his creation.

TURKEY SOUNDS

U.S. artist Jay Jones created "audio sculptures" by playing the sounds of gobbling turkeys to Christmas shoppers in West Yorkshire, England.

EDIBLE EXHIBITION

A show at an art gallery in Brighton, England, gave visitors a chance to eat the exhibits in 2005. "The Lost Apple Field" presented 700 varieties of apples to highlight how people have lost touch with traditional farming.

BATTERY-POWERED

Scientists at Japan's Tokyo Institute of Technology have invented an airplane powered solely by 160 tiny AA batteries. The 97-lb (44-kg) plane, with a 100-ft (30-m) wingspan, flew 1,283 ft (391 m) in one minute during tests in 2006, in what was thought to be the world's first household battery-powered takeoff.

STEAM GRAMOPHONE

Music-lover and steam-train enthusiast Geoff Hudspith from Dorset, England, has created what he claims is the world's first steam-powered gramophone... just so that he could play his collection of old 78 rpm records. It took him four years to build but cost him less than $200 because he used scrap metal.

MINI MASTERS

At the Smithsonian Institute in Washington, D.C., a mini art exhibition featured 1,122 tiny artworks measuring an average of 3 x 4 in (7.6 x 10 cm).

CHAMBER MUSIC

An American firm has invented a new iPod accessory that combines the portable music player with a toilet-roll holder so you can enjoy your favorite tunes while in the bathroom.

Calligrapher Zhang Kesi writes the Chinese character "Long" (dragon) on a banner measuring 190 ft (58 m) long and 92 ft (28 m) wide in China. Kesi used a brush 18 ft (5.5 m) long and 6 ft 9 in (2 m) in diameter. The total length of the character stroke is 469 ft (143 m).

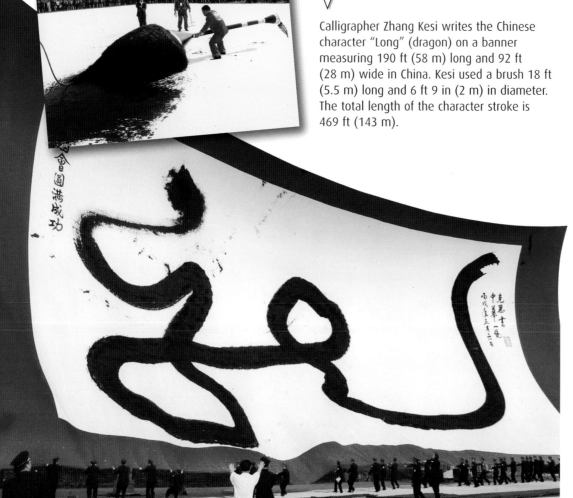

Cartoon Mania

CARTOON MANIA HAS GRIPPED MANY RIPLEY'S FANS OVER THE YEARS. AT THE HEIGHT OF THEIR ENORMOUS POPULARITY IN THE 1930s, ROBERT RIPLEY'S BELIEVE IT OR NOT! CARTOONS HAD MORE THAN 80 MILLION READERS DAILY.

FRANK S. NAROKI FROM CLEVELAND, OHIO, COLLECTED ENOUGH BELIEVE IT OR NOT! CARTOONS FROM 1929 TO 1932 TO WALLPAPER HIS ENTIRE BEDROOM. THE LAST THING HE SAW AT NIGHT AND THE FIRST THING WHEN HE AWOKE, HIS COLLECTION OF BELIEVE IT OR NOT! CARTOONS UNDOUBTEDLY GAVE HIM A NEW TOPIC OF CONVERSATION OVER BREAKFAST EVERY MORNING!

UNBELIEVABLE DUMMY

Walter Cunningham, seen here in 1944, made his ventriloquist's dummy out of papier-mâchéd Ripley's *Believe It or Not!* cartoons, and used the dummy in his act for more than 30 years.

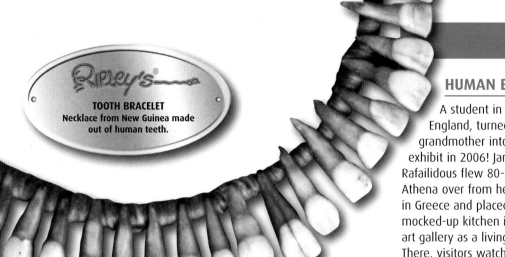

Ripley's®
TOOTH BRACELET
Necklace from New Guinea made
out of human teeth.

HUMAN EXHIBIT

A student in Yorkshire, England, turned her own grandmother into an art exhibit in 2006! Janis Rafailidous flew 80-year-old Athena over from her home in Greece and placed her in a mocked-up kitchen in a Leeds art gallery as a living sculpture. There, visitors watched Athena tidying up, preparing food, and even doing some knitting.

BARBIE MUTILATOR

There is a good reason why San Francisco artist Sue Wandell is known as the "Barbie Mutilator." Wandell produces works of art by chopping off the heads of Barbie dolls and replacing them with household objects. Among her creations are "Hammerhead Barbie" (where the doll's head is replaced by that of a metal hammer), "Vanity Barbie" (who has a mirror for a head) and "Bar Fly Barbie" (whose head is a removable pouring top for bottles of alcohol).

ASH FOREST

As part of a degree show at Camberwell College of Arts in London, England, student Emma Fenelon glazed five ceramic trees with human ashes. She had advertised on the Internet for volunteers to donate the remains of their loved ones for the project.

COLD COMFORT

A company in Alabama has developed a talking refrigerator magnet that berates dieters when they open the fridge to snack!

HORNET MOUNTAIN

In 1999, Yoshikuni Shiozawa of Nagano, Japan, created a model of Mount Fuji 12 ft (3.6 m) high by joining together 160 hornet nests. The finished sculpture contained no fewer than 160,000 hornets.

SAND PAINTING

In September 2005, more than 200 people made a sand painting measuring 46 x 52 ft (14 x 16 m) of "Fun in the Sun" at Jersey, Channel Islands, U.K. Half a ton of sand was mixed with poster paint to create 17 different colors. The dyed sand was then sprinkled onto hardwood sheets over areas of the design that had been covered with glue.

MINUTE FLAG

Jang-Bae Jeon and Carlo Foresca, students at the University of Texas in Dallas, have created a likeness of the American flag so small it would take 14 of them to span the width of a human hair. Using nanotechnology, they made an image of the flag—complete with all 50 stars and 13 stripes—that is just seven microns tall, compared to the 100-micron width of a human hair.

CANDY-WRAPPER ▷ COUTURE

Klavdiya Lyusina, from the village of Tsaryov in Russia, proudly models the skirt, jacket, headscarf, and bag that she made herself, out of candy wrappers. Klavdiya has been making clothes and accessories from these bright wrappers for the past 20 years.

STATE PAINTER

Artist Scott Hagan of Belmont County, Ohio, traveled 65,000 mi (105,000 km) through the state using 645 gal (2,445 l) of paint and 100 brushes to paint the state logo on 88 different barns in celebration of the Ohio bicentennial.

MUD ART

HOT ICE

Scott Wilson of Cary, North Carolina, has created an ice cream that is made with three kinds of peppers and two types of hot sauce. The product, Cold Sweat, is so hot that customers must sign a waiver before tasting it.

REPLICA ARK

Inspired by the biblical story of Noah, Dutchman Johan Huibers spent 15 months building a wooden ark 230 ft (70 m) in length that he planned to fill with farmyard animals, and sail to several cities in The Netherlands.

ROBOT CONDUCTOR

In 2004, a humanoid robot 23 in (58 cm) tall conducted the Tokyo Philharmonic Orchestra in a performance of Beethoven's 5th Symphony.

CHOPPER MOWER

C.G. Mouch of Brusly, Los Angeles, fitted the front end of a 750cc Honda motorcycle to the rear end of a lawn mower to create a "chopper mower"—so that he could mow in style at speeds of up to 10 mph (16 km/h)!

Artist Angela Findlay from London, England, certainly gets her hands dirty in the name of art. She paints pictures with mud taken from the banks of England's Severn River. Angela collects mud in buckets before taking it back to her studio to mix with sand and acrylic paints. She then paints onto large canvases with her hands and fingernails.

ORIGAMI EXPERT

Devin Balkcom, a student at Carnegie Mellon University in Pittsburgh, Pennsylvania, developed a robot that can do origami, the ancient Japanese art of paper sculpture.

JUNK CREATIONS

Freeman Loughridge of Ardmore, Oklahoma, uses discarded junk to create quirky sculptures. Bicycle parts and springs form the basis for a flowering garden trellis, while an old army helmet has been converted into a flamingo! Loughridge says of his whimsical creations: "I'm very serious about not being serious."

FLOWER POWER

In September 2005, a bouquet of more than 150,000 roses was created at a shopping mall in Frankfurt, Germany.

ROBOTIC TASTER

Japanese engineers claim to have developed a robotic wine taster that is capable of distinguishing between 30 different varieties of grape!

CHIN POWER

Owen Orthmann of Minnesota, paralyzed from the neck down, modified a crossbow so that it can be easily loaded, aimed, and fired without the use of arms or legs. Instead he fires it with his chin.

BUTTON COUTURE ▷

In 1936, Owen Totten of Mount Erie, Illinois, modeled a suit that he'd covered with 5,600 buttons—no two of which were alike.

⚠ ART AWASH

Volunteers stand at the water's edge and read newspapers to form a "human sculpture" on Manly Beach, Sydney, Australia. Artist Andrew Baines called for men, women, and children on September 2, 2006, to meet him at the beach at daybreak to form this sculpture. Baines said his live work had been inspired by a revelation as a child on the London Underground at rush hour, where he faced a sea of "corporate battery hens."

ILLUMINATED SLIPPERS

Trips to the refrigerator for a middle-of-the-night snack could be safer thanks to U.S. inventor Doug Vick who has devised a pair of slippers with lights. The slippers have powerful flashlights in the toes that shine a beam of light for distances of up to 25 ft (7.6 m). When the slippers are removed, a timer means that the light stays on long enough to enable the wearer to climb back into bed!

GUIDO'S HANDICRAFT

Italian artist Guido Daniele has given a new meaning to finger-painting. Instead of working on canvas, he uses pencil and watercolors on human hands to create incredible portraits of animals and birds such as cheetahs, elephants, crocodiles, and toucans. Daniele, who used to paint human bodies for advertising campaigns, takes up to ten hours to produce his handicraft. This means that his models not only need big hands but a lot of patience as well.

EYEBALL MOUSE

Chinese high-school student Zhou Chen of Nanjing has invented a special computer that can be operated by the user simply moving his or her eyeballs. The "eyeball mouse," as he calls it, enables users to click and, for example, open a website just by looking at the screen and moving their eyes.

SCRABBLE SCULPTURE

Scottish artist David Mach created a sculpture of a woman 8 ft (2.4 m) tall from 4,200 regular Scrabble tiles. The sculpture, entitled "Myslexia," was displayed in Sussex, England, in 2006 and the letters on the tiles were calculated to be worth more than 76,000 points!

MIGHTY MOUSETRAP

Students at the Art Institute in Fort Lauderdale, Florida, built a mousetrap 12 ft (3.6 m) long and weighing more than 600 lb (270 kg).

SAVED DISKS

Artist Tom Dukich of Spokane, Washington, saved on-line software disks for 10 years—enough to fill a 30-gal (115-l) garbage can—then created a giant sculpture out of them.

EAGLE-EYED

Nuclear scientist Bob Gibb and engineer Tom Chapman of New Brunswick, Canada, have developed special sunglasses that help golfers locate their lost golf balls.

SPOTS BEFORE THE EYES!

In August 2006, the New South Wales Art Gallery in Sydney, Australia, played host to a mind-boggling work of art that had visitors literally seeing spots before their eyes. Australian artist Nike Savvas created the piece, entitled "Atomix—Full of Love, Full of Wonder," from more than 50,000 polystyrene balls. The balls vibrate with the wind from ten fans to represent the hot shimmering colors found in the Australian outback.

13

IN DEPTH
PICK OF THE BUNCH

San Franciscan artist Steven J. Backman, goes through more than 10,000 toothpicks a year creating his world-renowned sculptures.

Where did your fascination with toothpicks come from?

❝When I was about five years old I made a DNA molecule from beans and toothpicks for a science project. I have a lot of patience when I work now, but I didn't back then— I got frustrated and hit it, and got a toothpick lodged in my hand. That's where it all began!❞

What is the most famous thing you have made?

❝An exact replica of San Francisco's Golden Gate Bridge, made 20 years ago. It's 13 ft long, and took 30,000 toothpicks, perfectly suspended without any cable or wire. It even lights up! It took about 2¼ years.❞

Do you have any other favorites?

❝My replicas of San Francisco cable cars, my abstract sculptures of masterworks such as the Mona Lisa or public figures such as President Bush... but above all, a 4½-ft-long radio-controlled yacht, covered with fiberglass resin for water resistance so it actually floats in water. It's my pride and joy—it was valued at $25,000 but I wouldn't sell it for a million dollars.❞

How does your work differ from that of model-makers?

❝Some people create big objects, but I create fine art. People don't always take it seriously because I use toothpicks and not bronze or plaster, but I want to create pieces—like my 2,330-toothpick interpretation of Rodin's The Thinker—that can be compared to Picasso or Rembrandt!❞

Do you wake up every morning and think: "Toothpick"?

❝I'm most creative when I'm asleep! I dream about things, and often get up in the middle of the night and start working on them.❞

What helps you to concentrate while you are working?

❝I used to work 24 hours straight without a break. These days I do about eight or ten hours a day. I work in total silence, not even a radio or a phone. I like to be alone.❞

What kinds of toothpicks do you use—and do they cost you a fortune?

❝I have a contract with a supplier—each piece I make generally requires at least 400 to 1,000 toothpicks. I use mainly blanks, which don't have the tapered ends. They're stronger. And lots of glue!❞

What toothpick challenge awaits you?

❝The hardest piece I made was the Empire State Building, with 7,470 toothpicks, because it was hollow. But the biggest challenge would be to make something life-sized. I want to make a car that will actually operate.❞

You have a motto—what is it?

❝It's 'The Essence of Patience'—to sit for hours on end you need extreme patience. Ironically, outside my work, I'm the most impatient person in the world—I don't even like to wait in line!❞

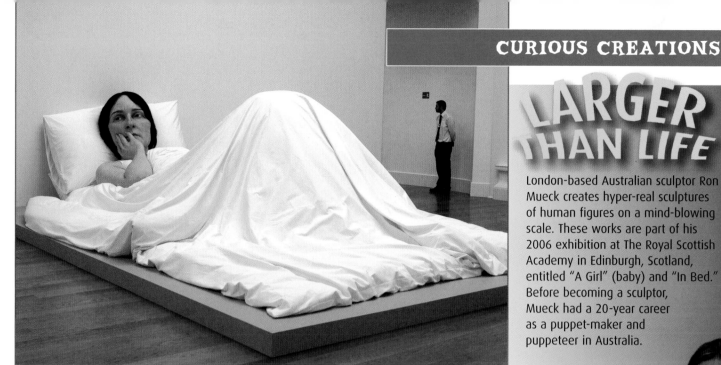

LARGER THAN LIFE

London-based Australian sculptor Ron Mueck creates hyper-real sculptures of human figures on a mind-blowing scale. These works are part of his 2006 exhibition at The Royal Scottish Academy in Edinburgh, Scotland, entitled "A Girl" (baby) and "In Bed." Before becoming a sculptor, Mueck had a 20-year career as a puppet-maker and puppeteer in Australia.

BALLOON SCULPTURE

New York balloon artists Larry Moss and Royal Sorell used 40,781 oblong balloons to create a huge soccer-related sculpture in which the goal, the players, and even the grass were all made of balloons! It took 640 man-hours to make. The players were 40 ft (12 m) tall and dressed in the colors of the national teams of Belgium and The Netherlands, the host nations for the 2000 European Soccer Championships.

JET CHAIR

Giuseppe Cannela of Bedfordshire, England, successfully attached a jet engine to the back of his mother-in-law's wheelchair, to reach speeds in excess of 60 mph (97 km/h)!

BRANCHING OUT

British artist Tim Knowles encourages trees to draw! He attaches pens to a thin branch, places a blank canvas at the end, and allows the wind to do the work.

DOG ON DISPLAY

For Vancouver's first Sculpture Biennale exhibition in 2006, passersby were encouraged to deposit random artistic items on shelves around the city. The objects placed included feathers, shoes, tree branches, and, briefly, a Chihuahua!

SNOW SHOW

At the National Screen Institute Film Festival held in Winnipeg, Manitoba, Canada, the audience sat outside in −22°F (−30°C) weather watching movies projected onto a giant block of snow!

CEMENT BOAT

A group of students from the University of Nevada spent a year working on an eight-man canoe made out of cement. The boat actually floats!

METAL CHEESE

Los Angeles sculptor Bruce Gray created a 25 x 43 x 29 in (64 x 110 x 74 cm) slice of cheese—in welded aluminum! "The Big Cheese," which has metal bubbles of various sizes, featured in the 2004 season finale of HBO's *Six Feet Under*.

FISH ART

Artist Carol Hepper of South Dakota creates sculptures using up to 200 dried fish skins! She collects the skins from fishing trips and fish processing facilities.

PLASTIC WRAPPER

People walking the streets of Washington, D.C., never know what they're going to find next.

It could be a parking meter dressed as a lollipop, a baby up a tree, a translucent dog on the shore, or a man buried head first in a utility box. These and many other strange sculptures that have cropped up around the city are the work of local street artist Mark Jenkins. Mark works primarily in packing tape and plastic wrap to create clear, lifelike molds. He first tried the technique at school when he covered a pencil in plastic wrap and tape, made an incision, and removed the pencil.

Twenty years later, in 2003, in a moment of boredom, he made a ball from clear tape. He went on to wrap the contents of his apartment before making a cast of his own body, which he placed in a dumpster.

Moving to Washington, his tape men soon began to spring up all over the city. Sometimes they were transparent, other times he would dress them in old clothes for added realism.

He has also created tape babies and animals, and has perched them in trees, on monuments, and with abandoned shopping carts.

IN DEPTH

What is your favorite piece of work?

"Right now, it's making the tape horses. They're fun to put out in nature and also in the city. I've been having a good time using them to turn traffic circles into merry-go-rounds."

Have you had any mishaps or "sticky moments" while creating a piece?

"I think about the physics of what I'm doing to make sure things—including me!—don't fall down from high places. I have specially customized tools to hang things from street lamps and trees."

What is the most challenging thing you dream of taping?

"I'd love to make a cast of Abraham Lincoln's head from Washington, D.C.'s Lincoln Memorial—every time I go I think how cool it would be to have it sitting in my living room when my friends come round. But the authorities won't let me get up there."

What is the worst reaction you've had to your work?

"Usually people don't know it's me—I'll put a black bag over the piece while I'm working, then whip it off and be gone in seconds. But once a guy saw me pulling a pair of legs out of a garbage bag and looked at me as if to say 'That doesn't look good!' —he didn't stick around!"

What will you do next?

"I'm working on a series called 'Legos'—fusing two bodies together to make creatures with two sets of legs and no heads running around the city. As long as I come up with new ideas that amuse me, I'll carry on."

PAPER HOUSES

Sherry Browne, an artist in Charleston, South Carolina, makes sculptures of houses and historical forts out of toilet paper!

PUMPKIN CARVER

Hugh McMahon of New York City makes his living sculpting fruits and vegetables. He charges $1,000 for a carved pumpkin or watermelon.

SUDOKU PAPER

A British company has catered for the craze in Japanese Sudoku numerical puzzles by producing special toilet paper with individual puzzles on each sheet!

FLASHY EARRINGS

Inventors in California have developed earrings that flash in time to the wearer's heartbeat.

MEAT ART

A 2006 exhibition in Ghent, Belgium, featured a coat made of beef steaks, along with a tent of bacon, and sleeping bags made from steaks. Artist Jan Fabre worked through the night to turn 220 lbs (100 kg) of steak, 33 lbs (15 kg) of minced meat, and a few miles of Parma bacon into art for his Temples of Meat exhibition. But the exhibit could be displayed only for three days before it began to rot. It was not the first time that Fabre had worked with meat. In 2000, he covered the columns of Ghent University in strips of bacon.

MEMORABLE KISSES

Artist Tino Sehgal created a show at the Art Gallery of Ontario in Toronto, Canada, in 2006 where pairs of dancers copied great kisses from the history of art. Visitors came into the gallery to find the dancers performing kisses as depicted by the likes of Rodin, Munch, and Klimt.

CHAIN REACTION

People are amazed when they see Wayne Simmons' ornate wooden carvings of eagles, bears, and pelicans. All the more so when they learn that whereas other artists choose more delicate methods of working, Simmons, of Louisa County, Virginia, carves his sculptures of animals and birds using a chain saw!

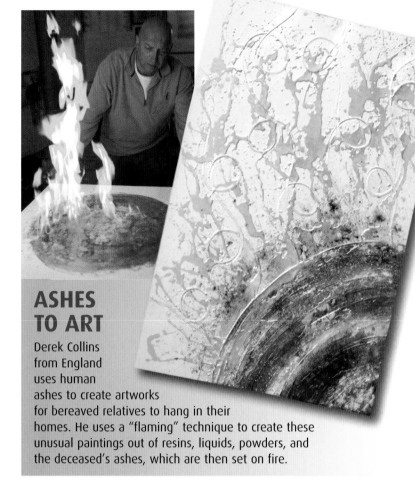

ASHES TO ART

Derek Collins from England uses human ashes to create artworks for bereaved relatives to hang in their homes. He uses a "flaming" technique to create these unusual paintings out of resins, liquids, powders, and the deceased's ashes, which are then set on fire.

PAINTS PANTS

Rachel Kice, an artist from Nashville, Tennessee, has made a career out of painting other people's pants. Kice gives the pants highly individual designs to transform ordinary clothes into fine-art pieces.

BABY BOTTLES

Steve Klein of Encino, California, produces hand-blown miniature wine bottles that are just over 1 in (2.5 cm) high. Each bottle is filled with 0.025 fl oz (0.75 ml) of wine, then corked, sealed, and labeled.

COMMUTE SUIT

To counter the heat wave that swept England in the summer of 2006, performance artist Liam Yeates invented a "commute suit" designed to make travel on the London Underground more bearable. The suit had colored spring-mounted balls to keep fellow commuters at least 6 in (15 cm) away, and a bowler hat with a flashing yellow light on top. Yeates also incorporated various gadgets useful for subway travel, including a fan in a briefcase, a built-in water bottle, and perfume bottles sewn into the shoulder pads of the suit to hide the smell of sweat on a particularly hot day.

TINY TESTAMENT

Using microlithography, three scientists at the Massachusetts Institute of Technology created a Bible measuring less than 0.2 sq in (1.3 sq cm) on a silicon tablet.

◁ BUTT PAINTING

Stan Murmer, an artist from Virginia, is the pioneer of "butt painting," which involves him sitting in paint and stamping his butt on a canvas to create images. He has created butt-print tulips, butterflies, and parrots by this method, among other things, and, believe it or not, he has actually sold some of his work.

Tractor Art

Australian artist Ando, who was trained as a mining engineer, has created a vast artwork of a smiling stockman that covers 1½ sq mi (4 sq km) of the Mundi Mundi Plains in New South Wales. Using a tractor to expose the red earth, it took Ando a year to create the artwork. The portrait is visible 1.2 mi (2 km) from above.

TURBO BEETLE

Ron Patrick wasn't content with quietly customizing his Volkswagen Beetle. He wanted something more dramatic, more explosive.

The California-based car computer designer wanted the wildest street-legal ride possible and spent four years making his creation safe to drive. He made several versions out of Styrofoam to get the layout and lighting right. The car has two engines—the production gasoline engine in the front driving the front wheels and the jet engine in the back. He says: "The idea is that you drive around legally on the gasoline engine and when you want to have some fun, you

Ron's jet engine once belonged to a navy helicopter, but has been converted for use in his Beetle.

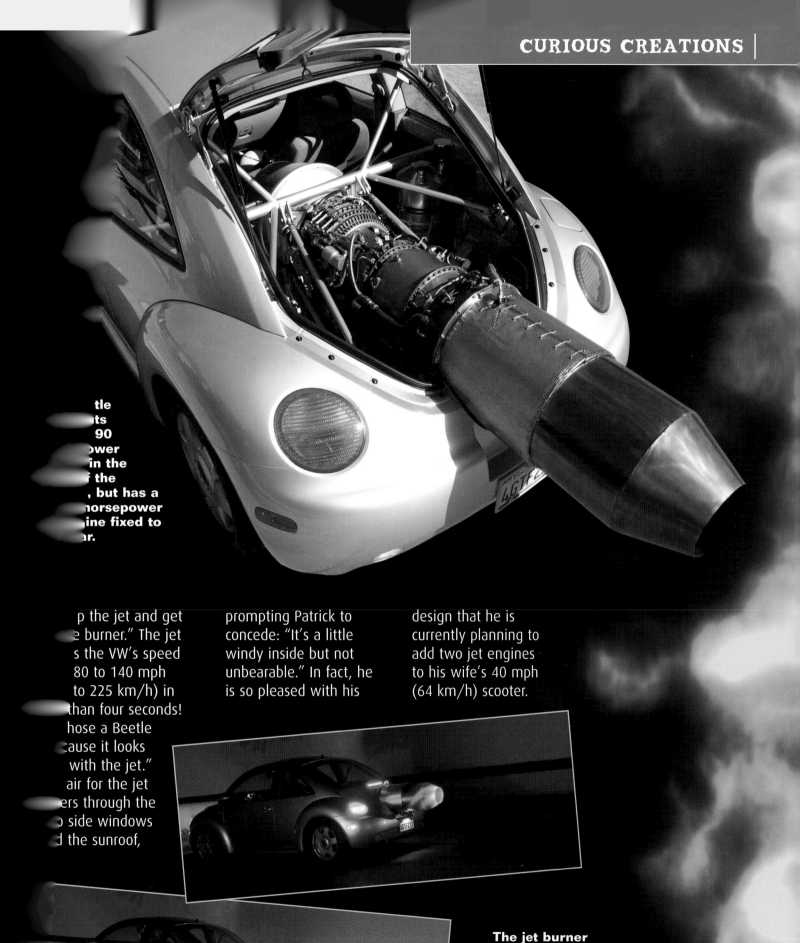

tle
ts
90
wer
in the
f the
, but has a
horsepower
ine fixed to
r.

p the jet and get
e burner." The jet
s the VW's speed
80 to 140 mph
to 225 km/h) in
than four seconds!
hose a Beetle
cause it looks
with the jet."
air for the jet
ers through the
o side windows
d the sunroof,

prompting Patrick to
concede: "It's a little
windy inside but not
unbearable." In fact, he
is so pleased with his

design that he is
currently planning to
add two jet engines
to his wife's 40 mph
(64 km/h) scooter.

**The jet burner
is particularly
eye-catching late
at night, which
is usually when
Ron tries it out.**

HAVING A BALL

Danny O'Connor, an artist from Lexington, Massachusetts, creates art using recycled objects, including Scotch tape and old record albums. But his favorite medium is balls, and over the years he has amassed no fewer than 22,000 discarded balls. One of his exhibits featured 17,000 found balls—tennis balls, footballs, squash balls, golf balls, beach balls, basketballs, and soccer balls—all arranged in a circle.

PUB PITCH

Pub landlord James Banbury is so crazy about soccer that he covered the interior of the Old Swan at Kibworth, Leicestershire, England, with turf for the 2006 World Cup. He laid turf on one of the bars, painted pitch markings on the grass, and turned the fireplace into a goal, complete with chalk-drawn goalposts and crossbar.

LONG CIGAR

Cigar makers in Tampa, Florida, have rolled a cigar that is 101 ft (31 m) long and weighs 53 lb (24 kg). It took Wallace and Margarita Reyes and their workers more than 75 man-hours over several weeks to craft the supersized smoke.

TOP MOSAIC

In celebration of the town's 950th anniversary in 2005, artists from Landesbergen, Germany, used more than 2¼ million bottle tops to create a mosaic that measured 325 x 209 ft (100 x 64 m). The mosaic was so big it had to be laid out on a soccer field.

STAMP HEAVY

In June 2006, artists Dmitry Shagin and Maksim Isayev delivered a postcard in St. Petersburg, Russia, that was 50 ft (15 m) long, weighed more than 123 lb (56 kg), and bore no fewer than 198 stamps!

ARCTIC BEER

A brewery in Greenland is producing beer by using water melted from the Arctic ice cap. Owners of the Inuit brewery—situated in Narsaq, a settlement 390 mi (628 km) south of the Arctic Circle—claim that the water is 2,000 years old and free of minerals and pollutants. The first consignment of the beer (which has 5.5% alcohol) is bound for the Danish market.

BARKING BELL

Gerrit Bruintjes of Oldenzaal, The Netherlands, has a doorbell that barks like a dog in memory of the family's German Shepherd that died a few years ago. It is so realistic that tax inspectors have twice ordered Bruintjes to get a dog licence because they think he has a dog in the house!

TINY FIELD

Using nanotechnology, a German scientist has created a soccer field so tiny that 20,000 of them could be put onto the tip of a single human hair! The minute creation even has all the details and markings of a real field.

HUMAN SCULPTURE

Mark Ho's handmade sculpture of the human body is made from bronze and stainless steel and stands 17 in (43 cm) high. Made from 920 different parts, including 101 pieces in each hand, it weighs 13 lbs (6 kg). It took Mark six years working on a prototype before he was happy with the final product. All joints are adjustable, which allows the figure to adopt an infinite number of positions.

INVERTED CHURCH

Visitors to Vancouver, Canada, in the summer of 2006 were stunned to see an upside-down church buried in the ground on its spire. Measuring 20 x 22 x 9 ft (6 x 6.7 x 2.7 m), it was made from steel, glass, and aluminum, and is called "Device To Root Out Evil." It is the work of New York-based sculptor Dennis Oppenheim.

ROBOT BARMAN

Students from the Technical University of Darmstadt in The Netherlands have created a robot that they claim can pour the perfect pint of beer! The robot, Hermann, is designed to pour the frothy German wheat beer at exactly the right angle.

FRIED FLAGS

Art student William Gentry of Clarksville, Tennessee, staged an exhibit of dozens of deep-fried American flags to protest against obesity. The flags were fried in peanut oil, egg batter, flour, and black pepper.

BIG BOOT

Igor Ridanovic of Los Angeles, California, has created the "Mono Boot," an extra-wide ski boot that holds both feet!

PLASTIC FANTASTIC

In a 2006 contest to make ingenious items from Tupperware, Evelyn Tabaniag of the Philippines designed a blue Tupperware evening bag, complete with lace lining and beaded bracelets for handles. And Stella Filippou from Greece modeled a Formula One race car entirely out of Tupperware items. The wheels were made from jello molds and potato mashers.

CONVERTED TROUGH

A 14-year-old Swiss boy has built a functioning submarine out of an old pig trough and other bits of farm equipment. Aaron Kreier has been working on the pedal-powered craft for four years and in July 2006 took it on a successful 15-minute maiden voyage.

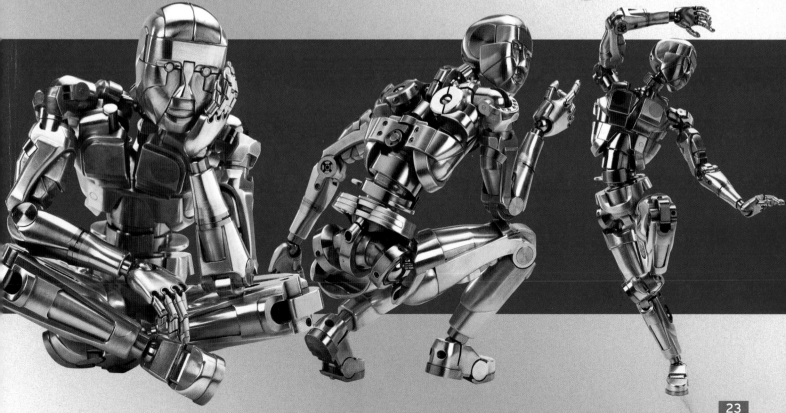

SNOW VILLAGE

A group of 200 Swiss enthusiasts built an igloo village 200 ft (60 m) wide, complete with snow church and piazza, on a frozen lake in 2006. Led by Lars Kienitz, they took 12 hours to build 100 igloos, many with kitchens, fireplaces, and ice sofas.

SOAP STATUE

New York artist Gary Sussman carved a scale replica of the Statue of Liberty, 12 ft (3.7 m) tall—out of soap. Sussman has also made a giant sculpture of Uncle Sam from a 5,000-lb (2,270-kg) block of soap.

COCKROACH BROOCH

A new creepy fashion accessory now on sale is the live giant Madagascar hissing cockroach. About 3 in (7.6 cm) in length, it is adorned with colored crystals that are glued in place on its hard outer shell. A small clasp attached to a silver chain allows the insect to roam around the wearer.

AUTO ROBOT

Blacksmith Sage Werbock from Hulmeville, Pennsylvania, has built a robot made entirely of welded car parts. The arms are made from shock absorbers, the chest from a speaker, and the feet from brake pads. The robot weighs more than 200 lbs (90 kg) and is 6 ft 9 in (2 m) tall. Werbock used his own body as a template, holding pieces of metal up to his arms and legs to get the proper ratios for his droid.

EIGHT-MILE SCARF

Helped by more than 1,000 volunteers, German woman Elfriede Blees knitted a scarf 8 mi (13 km) long to commemorate the 2006 World Cup. The scarf, which featured the flags of all 32 nations competing in the soccer tournament, used some 70,000 balls of wool, worth around $30,000.

BUTTER FIGURES

For an exhibition at the Pennsylvania Farm Show, sculptor Jim Victor spent a week in a refrigerator carving 900 lbs (400 kg) of butter into models of two life-size cows and the late chocolate magnate Milton Hershey! Victor, from Conshohocken, Pennsylvania, has also made pigs, a tractor, and a Harley-Davidson from chocolate, and dinosaurs and cars from cheese.

△ CAN DO

In 2006, 55 cities built 500 structures in the Canstruction competition. Works of art, such as this frog, were made from up to 20,000 full cans of food. A variety of can sizes and shapes were used, with the product labels serving as the color pallet. Other materials permitted included clear tape, magnets, elastic bands, and wire.

LEONARDO DA VINCI IN NAILS ▽

Albanian artist Samir Strati spent almost a month creating a huge 3-D nail mosaic portrait of Leonardo da Vinci using some 500,000 industrial nails. His work, measuring an impressive 86 sq ft (8 sq m), was displayed at the International Center of Culture in the Albanian capital Tirana, in August 2006.

SECRET GARDENING

Members of the Guerilla Gardening Movement in England secretly plant gardens and shrubbery in run-down urban areas under cover of darkness.

TREE MESSAGES

Artist Antje Krueger held an exhibition in Berlin, Germany, that consisted of notes and messages that had been put up on trees and lampposts in her neighborhood.

Way to go!

K. Sudhakar from Hyderabad, India, designed his first bicycle at the age of 14, before going on to create 150 different types of cars, dune buggies, and go karts, such as the camera, cricket ball, cup and saucer, and helmet. He has also designed more than 30 different bi- and tricycles, including a bicycle measuring only 6 in (15 cm) high, and a tricycle 41 ft 7 in (12.7 m) tall. All his models are fully working.

HAMBURGER

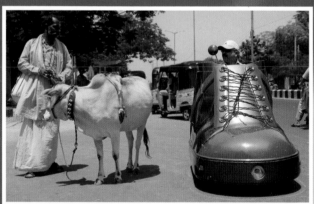

TOILET

SHOE

TRICYCLE

BED

CRICKET BALL

RESEARCH COUP

A flock of 20 pigeons wearing cell phone backpacks were employed to monitor California air pollution in 2006. Each pigeon carried a cell phone with a satellite tracking chip and air pollution sensor, enabling data on air quality to be transmitted via text messages. The birds also had miniature cameras tied around their necks to record aerial pictures of environmental black spots.

BLINKING MOUSE

Dmitry Gorodnichy, an inventor from Ottawa, Canada, has developed a computer mouse controlled by nose movements and blinking. He calls the nose-steered mouse a "nouse" and blinking the left or right eye twice takes the place of left or right mouseclicks.

TIRE TREE

British sculptor Douglas White has created a 16-ft (4.8-m) palm tree made from blown-out truck tires in the middle of a rainforest in northern Belize.

OUTSIZE COW

Harvey Jackson spent over 18 months and 220 gal (833 l) of paint creating a 220 x 56 ft (67 x 17 m) mural at Gillette, Wyoming. It depicted a tractor, a train, and a cow, representing the town's major industries. The cow alone is larger than George Washington's face on Mount Rushmore.

CHEESE CHURCH

In Edam, The Netherlands, there is a 1:10 scale model of the town's great church made out of 10,000 balls of Edam cheese.

FINGER PAINTING

Elizabeth McLeod and Amanda Riley, both ten from Snelville, Georgia, created a giant finger painting that measured 3,100 sq ft (290 sq m).

BATHROOM PLAY

A play in Sao Paulo, Brazil, in 2006 was staged in a theater bathroom! Only 30 audience members could fit inside the bathroom and they had to stand during the half-hour show.

TINY TREASURES

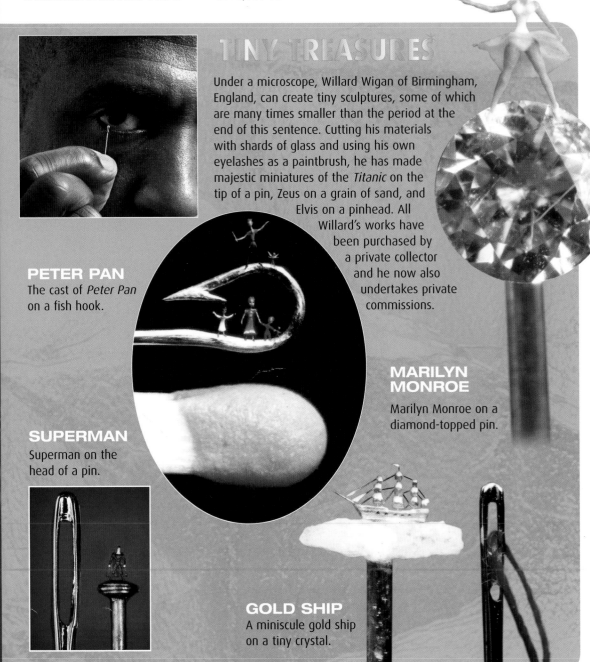

Under a microscope, Willard Wigan of Birmingham, England, can create tiny sculptures, some of which are many times smaller than the period at the end of this sentence. Cutting his materials with shards of glass and using his own eyelashes as a paintbrush, he has made majestic miniatures of the *Titanic* on the tip of a pin, Zeus on a grain of sand, and Elvis on a pinhead. All Willard's works have been purchased by a private collector and he now also undertakes private commissions.

PETER PAN
The cast of *Peter Pan* on a fish hook.

SUPERMAN
Superman on the head of a pin.

MARILYN MONROE
Marilyn Monroe on a diamond-topped pin.

GOLD SHIP
A miniscule gold ship on a tiny crystal.

SHEDBOATSHED

British artist Simon Starling won the 2005 Turner Prize for converting a shed into a working boat and then back into a shed! He found his wooden shack in the Swiss town of Schweizerhalle and, after turning it into a boat, he paddled 7 mi (11 km) down the River Rhine to Basel, where he rebuilt it. In a previous artwork he used the waste water produced by a self-built electric bicycle during a ride across a Spanish desert to create a cactus painting.

PETITE PICASSO

Phoenix Perego of Ormond Beach, Florida, sees her paintings sell for anything between $50 and $100. And that's no mean feat considering she is only 2½ years old! She has created more than 15 works and, according to her father, who is himself a professional artist, she likes to paint in her diaper.

ICE CARVING

Residents of Arlberg, Austria, created a near full-size replica of their town hall out of 176,500 cu ft (5,000 cu m) of snow and ice. Led by sculptor Christoph Strolz, volunteers spent hundreds of hours painstakingly carving out the 46-ft-high, 65-ft-long (14 x 20 m) building on the side of a mountain.

MINI MOBILE

Jan Krutewicz of Munster, Illinois, built a working telephone that is smaller than a human thumb.

STONEHENGE REPLICA

When he died, Al Sheppard of Hunt, Texas, was cremated and had his ashes spread about the half-sized replica of Stonehenge that he had built on his property.

EGGSCLUSIVE ART △

Many years of training have enabled Wang Jinyi from Tianjin, China, to develop his considerable skill in egg carving. He carves a variety of subjects ranging from characters in ancient Chinese legends to the mascots for the Beijing 2008 Olympics.

ROME RECREATED

Using 10,000 tons of special river sand imported from The Netherlands, 60 artists created sand sculptures depicting the glory of Ancient Rome. Among the 200 sculptures at the exhibition, which opened in Brighton, England, in summer 2006, were the Pantheon, the Colosseum, and Emperor Augustus.

NOTE HUNTERS

Davy Rothbart of Ann Arbor, Michigan, is the editor of the magazine *Found*, which prints letters, photos, drawings, and notes that he and others have found on the ground.

BEACH SCULPTURE

In 1991, a sand sculpture an astonishing 16.4 mi (26.4 km) long was built by more than 10,000 volunteers at Myrtle Beach, South Carolina.

HEAVY EGG

Twenty-six chocolate makers took eight days and used 50,000 chocolate bars to make an edible chocolate egg that measured 27 ft 3 in (8.3 m) tall, 21 ft (6.4 m) wide and weighed 4,299 lb (1,950 kg). Metal scaffolding with wooden panels was used to create a "shell" to support the egg, which went on display at Englewood Cliffs, New Jersey.

CARTON CARTOGRAPHER

Skip Hunsaker of Coos Bay, Oregon, created a topographical map of his home county using cigarette cartons! A specialist in unusual materials, he also made miniature poodle figures from myrtlewood nuts.

FALLEN HOUSE

There is something strange on the roof of Austria's Viennese Museum of Modern Art—an upside-down house. In fact, it is a sculpture by Erwin Wurm and, although it is supposed to look as if the house has fallen from the sky and landed on the museum, it actually took two large cranes to lift it into place.

DUCT LOVE

Something to Do, a band in Waukesha, Wisconsin, won $2,500 in a songwriting contest by writing a love song about duct tape!

PENNY PILE

Artist Gerald Ferguson created a work of art at a gallery in Halifax, Nova Scotia, Canada, that consisted of a pile of one million pennies, worth $10,000.

CARDBOARD PIANO

Researchers in a Swedish packaging company have made a working grand piano out of cardboard.

△ HEART-SHAPED TREE

This romantically shaped tree was photographed growing out of solid rock in Manitoba, Canada.

△ ROTTEN ART

Rotten tomatoes, moldy bread, and decomposing fruits formed the centerpieces of an art exhibition in England in January 2000. The exhibits were the work of Canadian artist Michael Smietana who wanted to highlight the amount of food wasted globally.

PIPE MUSIC

Mike Silverman of Walnut Creek, California, makes music playing a galvanized steel pipe that is 7 ft (2.1 m) long and fitted with a bass and cello string.

GINGERBREAD HOUSE

A gingerbread house standing over 67 ft (20.4 m) tall was designed by Roger Pelcher in Bloomington, Minnesota, in 2006. It took a team of builders nine days to create the cookie domicile, which contains 14,250 lb (6,464 kg) of gingerbread, 4,750 lb (2,155 kg) of icing, and more than one ton in candy embellishments.

POTATO LONGHOUSE

Over a layer of glue and cardboard, Washington State artist Marilyn Jones created an authentic-looking model of a longhouse from steak fries, shoe-string potatoes, hashbrowns, and instant mashed potato.

FLORAL SCULPTURE

A floral sculpture measuring 249 x 86 ft (75 x 26 m) and resembling a strip of Aspirin tablets was constructed in one week by nearly 2,000 people in Jakarta, Indonesia, in 1999.

GUM ARTIST

In 2004, German artist Heidi Hesse made a life-sized Humvee sculpture 16 ft (5 m) long from gum balls!

CHEESY PERFUME

The British makers of the pungent Stilton blue cheese have launched their own perfume, Eau de Stilton. It claims to "re-create the earthy and fruity aroma" of the cheese "in an eminently wearable perfume."

VARNISHED GOURDS

Larry Ray of Gulfport, Mississippi, paints and sculpts gourds. His beautifully decorated creations are finished with two coats of varnish and one coat of paste wax.

GINGERBREAD TOWN

Sven Grumbach re-created the entire town of Rostock, Germany, out of gingerbread. The 4,300-sq-ft (400-sq-m) model was made using 1,760 lb (800 kg) of flour, 705 lb (320 kg) of honey, 880 lb (400 kg) of almonds, 175 lb (80 kg) of raisins, and 2,400 eggs.

FAVORITE VIEW

Artist William A. Bixler of Anderson, Indiana, created 5,000 paintings—all of the same scene, a swimming spot on the Brandyvine River.

△ SECRET HEART

A heart-warming surprise greeted loggers (and their young helper) when they cut down this tree to find a perfect heart within its trunk.

CUDDLY CAR

Art student Lauren Porter has created a sports car you could pull over very stylishly in—a Ferrari knitted from wool! Lauren, from Hampshire, England, spent ten months making the full-size replica for her honors degree project, using 12 mi (19 km) of yarn. Supported by a steel frame, the red bodywork consists of 250 squares of garter stitch. The windows are V-shaped stocking stitch and the Ferrari horse badge is hand-embroidered.

FIZZY MONSTER

At the 2006 Kentucky Art Car Weekend, Lewis Meyer decorated the front of his Nissan truck with a sea monster made out of soda bottle caps.

FLOATING BED

Dutch architect Janjaap Ruijssenaars has spent six years developing a floating bed that hovers 15¾ in (40 cm) above the ground through magnetic force. Magnets built into the floor and into the bed repel each other, pushing the bed up into the air. Thin steel cables tether the bed in place. The bed, which was inspired by the cult film *2001: A Space Odyssey*, has a price tag of around $1,500,000!

THE CANDY MAN

Jason Mecier is a celebrity portrait artist with a difference. Whereas other artists depict the rich and famous in traditional paints, San Francisco-based Mecier creates celebrity mosaics from household odds and ends or food products. Starting out with beans and noodles, he has progressed to doing candy portraits of, among others, Pamela Anderson, Christina Aguilera, Dolly Parton, and the Spice Girls. He has re-created Martha Stewart entirely out of vegetables, Demi Moore from dog food, Marilyn Manson in yarn, Mariah Carey in her favorite make-up, Billy Bob Thornton out of cigarette cartons, and Sigmund Freud from tablets and pills.

Fitting Forms

Britt Savage, a singer from Nashville, Tennessee, used mostly pink child and dependent care 1040A forms and individual tax forms to create this dress in 2009 to wear on stage.

Using a shredder to make the thin strips, she then wove them together to make the center of the dress and glued them to the bottom to create the skirt.

◬ TAPAGAMI TOWN

Daniel Schieble from California is a "Tapagami" artist—he uses only masking tape and painter's tape. In 2007, he started working on this masking tape city entitled "Atlas Losing his Grip on the World." After only a few years it measures about 2,000 sq ft (186 sq m). He refers to his art as a self-regenerating sculpture, as he works on it nearly every night. So far, he has used approximately 14 mi (23 km) of masking tape.

UV TATTOOS

This ultraviolet tattoo is the handiwork of Richie Streate, a Californian tattoo artist who specializes in UV tattoos. The tattoos are completely invisible in regular light, once the scarring heals after about a year, but come to life under UV light used in clubs and bars.

HOPPING MAD

A company in Los Angeles developed a motorized pogo stick powered by a single two-cycle engine that gets 30,000 hops to the gallon.

RECYCLED PURSES

Saroj Welch of Louisiana crochets recycled plastic grocery bags into purses, then donates the proceeds to charity.

SALVAGE SHIP

The USS *New York*, a transport ship, is being built with 24 tons of steel salvaged from New York City's World Trade Center buildings.

SMALL WRITING

A.B. Rajbansh of India handwrote the U.S. Constitution in a 124-page book that measures only ¾ in (2 cm) in height.

TINY GUN

Mark Koscielski, a gunshop owner in Minneapolis, Minnesota, has created a double-barrel shotgun the size of a credit card.

PLANE LAMPS

Designer John Erik of Montreal, Canada, makes furniture and lamps out of discarded airplane parts, including engine turbines.

WASTE MAN

British sculptor Antony Gormley has created a sculpture 82 ft (25 m) high called *Waste Man* in Margate, England. The figure is made entirely from waste materials, including chairs, wardrobes, pictures, old rope, and toilet seats.

SHINY SHOES

Berlin artist Cihangir Gumustukmen uses recycled tin cans to make shoes. Whether they are slippers, sandals, stilettos, or platform shoes, he can create them to form works of art.

LONG BIBLE

A Bible written on a piece of silk 16,427 ft (5,007 m) long—that's about 3 mi (4.8 km)—was exhibited in Beijing, China, in 2006. The longest Bible in the world, it consists of 50 volumes written in 900,000 Chinese characters and is perfect in every detail.

LIGHT AIRCRAFT

Alexander van de Rostyne created the Pixelito, a tiny helicopter that is controlled by infrared light. The invention, which was displayed in Brussels, Belgium, weighs a mere ¼ oz (6.9 g).

COW PARADE

A 2006 Cow Parade in Lisbon, Portugal, featured a herd of life-size fiberglass cows over which artists painted colorful, individual designs.

△ GILLETT'S GULLET

Chris Gillett took a photograph of every meal he ate for a year! He took a digital photo of every breakfast, lunch, dinner, and snack he devoured in 2005—a total of 2,550 images. He then arranged them in a 16-ft (4.8-m) collage and exhibited them at a gallery near his home in Wiltshire, England. He said he got the idea after sending his wife a photo of a burger he ate in Los Angeles.

FEMININE ROADSTER

Anita Dugat-Greene of Belton, Texas, has turned her 1997 Ford Taurus into a monument to women. The car is covered in thousands of buttons, numerous images of the Virgin Mary, and multicultural Barbie dolls.

CAR COFFIN

Jose Gomez of Ilhavo, Portugal, built a wooden replica of his Mercedes 220 CDI car. He plans to be buried in it!

CARD SIGN

In July 2006, Bryan Berg of Spirit Lake, Iowa, used 500 decks of playing cards, 1,800 poker chips, 800 dice, and several tubes of Superglue to build a replica of the "Welcome to Las Vegas" sign. It took him 450 hours—that's nearly 19 days.

BREAD STATUE

Chilean artist Constanza Puente made a life-size statue of herself out of bread. When she placed the sculpture on a Santiago park bench in 2006, it quickly proved popular with pigeons.

SWEET CAR

The tastiest sight at the 2006 Baton Rouge, Louisiana, Art Car Parade was Amy James's OREO Speedwagon. It was a Ford Contour decorated with 30 bags of Oreo cookies.

COLORFUL SARI

A silk sari made in India has no fewer than 164,492 colors. The Seven Wonders of the World were brought to life on the border of the sari, which took 15 weavers more than 45 days to complete.

STRAW CHURCH

Farmers Will Morris and his son Tim spent two days creating a straw replica of an English village church in 2006, only for vandals to burn it down. The model of St. Mary's Priory Church in Deerhurst, Gloucestershire, stood 40 ft (12.2 m) tall, weighed 30 tons, and was made from 110 bales of straw.

ICE TOWER

Using 45 tons of ice, ten carvers spent 1,440 man-hours creating an ice sculpture that measured 40 ft (12.2 m) tall in Dubai in 2006. The sculpture is a mini version of the Burj Al Alam, which, when completed in 2012, will be one of the world's tallest commercial towers.

POPCORN MICKEY

Sculptors have created a giant model of Mickey Mouse as the Sorcerer's Apprentice... out of popcorn. The model, which stands 19 ft 8½ in (6 m) tall, was created at Disneyland's California Adventure Theme Park using prefabricated blocks of popcorn that were glued together.

TROLLEY RESCUER

British sculptor Ptolemy Elrington rescues supermarket carts that have been dumped in rivers and lakes and turns them into beautiful water wildlife creations. He saws up the carts and welds them into new shapes at his Brighton studio. Each sculpture takes him up to three weeks to complete. Among his works are a frog with bulging eyes (made from the cart's wheels), a dragonfly with a 6-ft (1.8-m) wingspan, and a kingfisher perched on top of a discarded cart.

DUAL PURPOSE

John and Julie Giljam of South Carolina made an amphibious motor home. The diesel-powered Terra Wind can reach speeds of more than 80 mph (130 kmph) on land and seven knots on the open water.

TV TREE

Lithuanian artist Gintaras Karosas has built a sculpture from around 3,000 old TV sets donated by the public. The sculpture, which looks like a tree when viewed from above, spans an area of 33,745 sq ft (3,135 sq m) and used 64,583 sq ft (6,000 sq m) of polythene, 7,535 sq ft (700 sq m) of bitumen cover, 3,178 cu ft (90 cu m) of wood, and 132 gal (500 l) of paint.

BEAD WATERFALL

To depict the annual salmon spawning, Bill and Clarissa Hudson constructed a cascading waterfall made from around 180,000 glass and crystal beads. The waterfall, which took two months to make, first went on display at Juneau, Alaska, in 1998.

▽ GREAT BALL OF STAMPS!

Fred W. Miller from Newark, New Jersey, made this 8½-lb (3.8-kg) ball from 75,000 used U.S. stamps in the 1940s. It measured an impressive 8 ft 9 in (2.7 m) in circumference.

CAR-COVERED CAR ▽

Installation artist James Robert Ford, based in London, England, spent three years creating this eye-catching car, which he completed in October 2006. For the work, James covered a Ford Capri with no less than 4,500 Matchbox® toy cars. He named it "General Carbuncle."

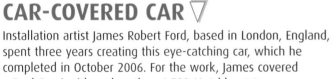

Index

ACKNOWLEDGMENTS

COVER (t/l) www.toothpickart.com, (b/l) Courtesy of private collector, (t/r) Mark Jenkins, (b/r) www.ronpatrickstuff.com; 4 Heather Jansch; 6–7 Heather Jansch; 8 (t) Newscom, (t/c) PA Photos; 9 (b) ChinaFotoPress/Getty Images; 11 (b) Rogulin Dmitry/UPPA/Photoshot; 12–13 (dp) Reuters/David Gray; 12 (t) 2daymedia; 13 (t) Ian Waldie/Getty Images; 14 www.toothpickart.com; 15 Jeff J Mitchell/Getty Images; 16–17 Mark Jenkins; 18 (b) Murmur, Stan. Sittin' Pretty [Anthropometric Monotype, Ashley Barlow] 2005, (t) 2daymedia; 19 AndoArt.com; 20–21 www.ronpatrickstuff.com; 22–23 Louis Lemaire © 2005 ZOHO Artforms; 24 (t) PA Photos, (b/l, b/c) Reuters/Arben Celi; 25 Stephen Boitano/Barcroft Media; 26 (fc) Christopher Hall/Fotolia.com, (t/l) David Burner/Rex Features, (t/r, c, b/l, b/r) Courtesy of private collector; 27 UPPA/Photoshot; 28–29 (c) 2daymedia; 28 (t) Philippe Hayes/AFP/Getty Images; 30 (t) Britt Savage, (b) www.dannyschieble.com; 31 (t) Richie Streate - The Dungeon Inc. USA, (b) UPPA/Photoshot; 32 Anna Barclay/Rex Features; 33 (b, b/r) Ben Phillips/Barcroft Media

All other photos are from Corel, PhotoDisc, Digital Vision and Ripley's Entertainment Inc.